CLASSROOM TO CAREER

MY JOB IN SCIENCE

BY
JOANNA BRUNDLE

PowerKiDS press

New York

Published in 2022 by The Rosen
Publishing Group, Inc.
29 East 21st Street, New York, NY 10010

© 2022 Booklife Publishing
This edition is published by arrangement
with Booklife Publishing

Edited by:
John Wood

Designed by:
Drue Rintoul

Cataloging-in-Publication Data

Names: Brundle, Joanna.
Title: My job in science / Joanna Brundle.
Description: New York : PowerKids Press,
2022. l Series: Classroom to career l
Includes glossary and index.
Identifiers: ISBN 9781725336469 (pbk.)
l ISBN 9781725336483 (library bound) l
ISBN 9781725336476 (6 pack) l
ISBN 9781725336490 (ebook)
Subjects: LCSH: Science--Vocational
guidance--Juvenile literature.
Classification: LCC Q147.B767 2022 l
DDC 502.3--dc23

Manufactured in the United
States of America

CPSIA Compliance Information: Batch #CWPK22.
For Further Information contact Rosen Publishing,
New York, New York at 1-800-237-9932.

Find us on 🅕 🅞

CONTENTS

WORDS THAT LOOK LIKE <u>THIS</u> CAN BE FOUND IN THE GLOSSARY ON PAGE 31.

CLASSROOM TO CAREER

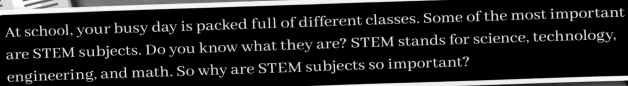

At school, your busy day is packed full of different classes. Some of the most important are STEM subjects. Do you know what they are? STEM stands for science, technology, engineering, and math. So why are STEM subjects so important?

USING STEM

The world moves very fast and it changes all the time. However, STEM can help us understand it. STEM subjects can inspire you to learn more about how the world works, and they might lead to you working in STEM. Lots of new STEM jobs are being created all the time and in all different areas. Who knows what you could be doing in the future? As well as helping you to find interesting work, studying STEM subjects will also help you to solve problems, make decisions, and work as part of a team.

JOB OR CAREER?

A job is something that you do to earn money. Many people stay in jobs for a short amount of time, and they don't always need training. A career is a lifelong work journey in an area that really interests you. People often need the right training for the right career.

Dentistry is a lifelong career that requires four years of dental school.

STEM subjects can help you get into an exciting career, whether you want to be an astronaut, doctor, or someone who makes video games. But remember that STEM subjects are important whatever you do. For example, many careers need you to have computer skills. In this book, we are going to look at science and some of the careers it might lead you to. We will be thinking about how you might spend your day and what qualifications and skills you might need.

Science experiments at school could lead to a career as a research scientist.

STEM CAREERS ARE FOR EVERYONE.

MARINE BIOLOGIST

Are you passionate about the natural world? Do you want to make a difference by protecting the environment for the future? Are you a great swimmer or diver? If so, working as a marine biologist could be the career for you. Marine biologists study our seas and oceans and the things that live there, including plants, fish, and other animals.

There are many roles within marine biology. Some people study tiny living things called algae, which can only be seen with a <u>microscope</u>. Others protect the giants of the sea, such as the blue whale. Marine biologists may work for charities or for <u>research laboratories</u>. Some work for zoos or sea life centers. Others are employed by companies that drill for oil and gas under the seabed. Marine biologists give these companies information about how to carry out work without damaging the environment.

This marine biologist is checking coral. Coral can be damaged by a rise in sea temperatures caused by <u>climate change</u>.

Marine biologists spend time both at sea and in a laboratory. At sea, they collect and store <u>specimens</u> and check on wildlife numbers, making note of where animals are and where they are going. In the laboratory, marine biologists use microscopes, computers, and other equipment to study specimens. For example, they might look at the effects of <u>pollution</u> on ocean creatures and plants.

These marine biologists are collecting seawater, which is then studied back at the laboratory.

To become a marine biologist, you will need a <u>degree</u> in marine biology, oceanography (the study of seas and oceans), or environmental science. As well as having a love of the natural world, you will also need to be a strong swimmer and be good at working in a team. You will need to work in a clear and careful way. You may need patience if the weather at sea is against you. It also helps if you like boats!

MARINE BIOLOGY GIVES PEOPLE THE CHANCE TO TRAVEL AROUND THE WORLD.

DOCTOR

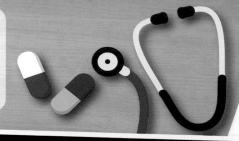

If you like the idea of helping people who are sick, then perhaps you should think of becoming a doctor. Doctors are specially trained people whose job it is to look at their patients, figure out what's wrong with them, and try to help them get better.

There are many different kinds of doctors. A GP (general practitioner) is often the first type of doctor people will call if they're ill. GPs treat everyday medical conditions, such as infections. They also send patients to hospitals for tests or special treatments. Hospital doctors may work on specialized hospital wards, in emergency rooms, or as surgeons. Some doctors are specially trained to care for children or the elderly. Other doctors are specially trained in particular areas of the body, such as the heart or brain.

GPs can see patients at a hospital or at home.

Surgeons are doctors who are specially trained to carry out operations.

It takes a long time to train as a doctor. You need to do very well in school to be able to train to be a doctor. You need to get an undergraduate degree, which takes about four years. Then, you need to go to medical school for about four years. Afterward, you work as a resident in a teaching hospital for three to seven years. Being a doctor can be a difficult career, but also a very important one. You could improve lots of people's lives, and even save lives too.

Some doctors work on air ambulances, helping people who have been in an accident.

As a doctor, you might also be able to work abroad because doctors are needed all over the world. Some choose to work for charities, caring for people in parts of the world that are hard to get to. Others work in disaster zones – for example, they might help people who have been caught in an earthquake.

This volunteer doctor is working in Africa.

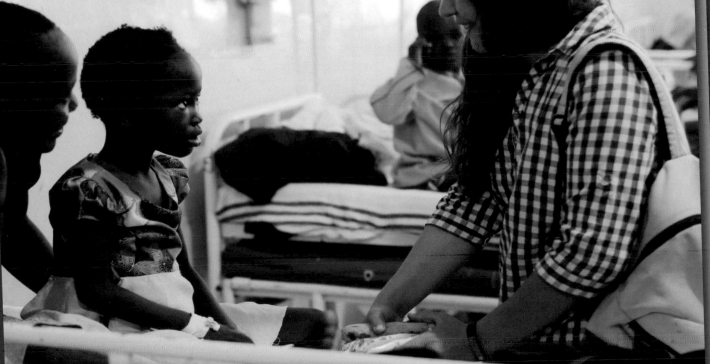

 DOCTORS NEED TO BE KIND AND CARING, AS WELL AS BEING GOOD LISTENERS. THEY MUST ALSO BE CALM AND ABLE TO DEAL WITH DIFFICULT SITUATIONS.

FORENSIC SCIENTIST

A forensic scientist helps to investigate crimes. They search for, collect, and study physical evidence from places where crimes have been carried out. Physical evidence includes fingerprints, blood, hair, pieces of clothing, paint, glass, tire marks, and anything that may have been used to start fires. A forensic scientist will use all these things to work out exactly what happened and who carried out the crime.

Hair being collected to study

At a crime scene, a forensic scientist will take photographs, make sketches, and keep written notes of where evidence was found. Each piece of evidence is stored and labeled before being taken to the laboratory. When a forensic scientist is at a crime scene, they wear protective clothing to prevent any contamination of the evidence and to protect themselves from anything dangerous.

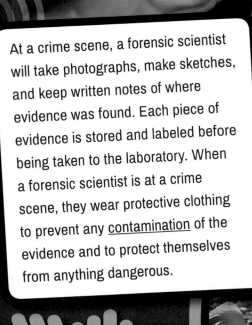

Protective clothing includes an all-in-one suit, hairnet, mask, gloves, and shoe covers.

SOME FORENSIC SCIENTISTS ARE SPECIALLY TRAINED TO FIND POISONS AND DRUGS.

Evidence that has been collected must be examined in the laboratory. It is often slow, detailed work. Forensic scientists need to work carefully and record all their findings. Physical evidence can link someone who is suspected of having carried out a crime to the crime scene, so there must be no mistakes.

As well as going to crime scenes and working in a laboratory, some forensic scientists also go to law courts to show their findings. They are called in as expert underlinewitnesses. This means that they can give an opinion about what they have found, as well as the facts.

Forensic scientists use fingerprint underlinedatabases to link fingerprints found at crime scenes to suspected criminals.

If being a forensic scientist sounds like the career for you, you will need a degree in biology, chemistry, or forensic science. Great attention to detail and being able to keep records is also needed.

RESEARCH SCIENTIST

Do you like finding out new things? Do you enjoy inventing and carrying out experiments of your own at home or at school? Perhaps the idea of making an important scientific discovery sounds interesting? What about finding a cure or new treatment for a disease or illness? If so, being a research scientist sounds like the career for you.

These scientists are carrying out research into new medicines.

Research scientists work in all sorts of areas of science. They can also work for lots of different types of employers. You might work for the government, or for a research laboratory that is owned by a company. You could work for an environmental agency or a company that makes and sells products that are sold in stores. Lots of people need research scientists.

Research scientists spend most of their time in the laboratory, where they plan and carry out experiments and record their results. They use special equipment, including computer software and powerful microscopes. Once they have looked carefully at their results, research scientists write reports that talk about what they have discovered.

A research specialist might use a special microscope like this.

As a research scientist, you might work away from the laboratory, for example collecting soil or water for testing. There are also chances to travel all over the world. You could go to <u>conferences</u>, where you might give a presentation to share your findings with other scientists.

To be a research scientist, you will need a degree in a science subject. A second degree called a master's degree is also helpful. As a person, you will need to be patient, determined, and good at working in a team.

A scientist collecting water

13

ZOOLOGIST

Are you an animal lover? Are you mad for monkeys, in love with llamas, or crazy about camels? If so, why not become a zoologist? Zoologists work with animals in their natural habitats and in places such as zoos and aquariums. They study what the animals do, as well as what they eat and how they have babies. They also study animal diseases.

The work of zoologists is interesting and always different. Some zoologists work to protect <u>endangered species</u> or look after habitats that are under threat.

Other zoologists choose to become specially trained to work with certain animals, such as reptiles, birds, or fish. Some run educational programs for adults and children visiting zoos and animal parks. Studying the effects of climate change on the number of animals and their movements is becoming more and more important.

YOU COULD BECOME A SPECIAL TYPE OF ZOOLOGIST, CALLED A PALEOZOOLOGIST. THEY STUDY ANIMAL <u>FOSSILS</u>.

If you choose to work with animals in places such as zoos and aquariums, you will be in charge of their food and their enclosures. Zoologists try to make sure that the animals' behavior can be as close as possible to their natural behavior in the wild.

Zoologists carry out research in the laboratory and outside in the world, where they collect and store specimens to be studied in the laboratory. This work could take you all over the world, including places that are difficult to get to, such as Antarctica.

You will need a degree in zoology, biology, environmental biology, or marine biology to become a zoologist. There are lots of people who want this career, so it might help to get some work experience. You will also need good computer skills, as you will be dealing with lots of data and using computer models to study the effects of human behavior on animal habitats.

SCIENCE TEACHER

The need for people in STEM careers is increasing all the time. How will we have enough people who are qualified to take on these careers? Step forward, science teachers of the future!

Science teachers encourage their students to be curious about the world around them and to think about how and why things happen. Science teaching begins when children start school. However, as a science teacher, you may find yourself teaching students of any age. Science teachers write and follow lesson plans, and they also assign and grade homework. They make sure that students are taught all that they need to know to pass exams.

Science teachers know about most areas of science, but they often know a lot about one particular subject. For example, they might teach an area of science called biology (the study of living things).

Goggles

Experiments are an important part of teaching science. Science teachers set up, perform, and explain experiments and encourage students to carry out their own. Laboratories can be dangerous places, so science teachers need to make sure their students understand how to work safely, for example using goggles when necessary.

Although science teachers spend most of their time in school, there are chances to work outside the classroom. For example, you might take students on field trips or to science presentations. It is important for you to keep up to date, so you may have to go to training sessions yourself.

To be a science teacher, you must have a science degree and be trained to teach children. You will need plenty of patience and enthusiasm and you must be good at talking to students, parents, and other staff.

FOOD SCIENTIST

We all need food to stay alive. But have you ever thought about how our food is produced? Who makes sure that it is safe and good for us to eat? This is the role of a food scientist.

Food scientists use their knowledge of science to study our food. They test its flavor, texture, and <u>nutritional value</u>. They look at the changes that take place in stored food and find new ways to keep it fresh and tasty. They also investigate ways of saving food companies time and money when making the food. Another important part of a food scientist's work is to test the safety of both uncooked ingredients and finished products. This is to make sure that the companies have followed the government's rules on food safety.

Food scientists spend most of their time working in laboratories.

Have you ever noticed the labels on food that tell you how many calories a food contains, and how much fat, sugar, and salt it is made up of? Labels often show how much is in one portion of the product. Food products are also stamped with "use by" or "best before" dates, which tell people when they can safely eat the food or enjoy it at its best. The labels also say which ingredients could cause an allergic reaction. For example, these ingredients could be eggs, wheat, or nuts. Food scientists work to find out all of this information.

Nutrition Facts

Serving Size 2 Rounded Scoops (4
Serving per Container 20

Amount Per Serving	
Calories 150 Calories from Fat 40	
% Daily Value*	
Total Fat 3.5g	5%
Saturated Fat 0g	0%
Trans Fat 0g	
Cholesterol 0mg	0%
Sodium 180mg	8%
Potassium 60mg	2%
Total Carbohydrate 15g	4%
Dietary Fiber 5g	20%
Sugars 1g	
Alcohol 5g	

You will need to work as part of a team.

If you'd like to be a food scientist, you'll need a degree in food science, chemistry, nutrition, or microbiology (the study of microbes).

19

RENEWABLE ENERGY SCIENTIST

Are you passionate about caring for the environment? Are you worried about climate change, and <u>fossil fuels</u> such as coal, oil, and gas? If you want to help make energy that is better for the planet, working as a renewable energy scientist could be right for you.

Wind farm

BURNING FOSSIL FUELS PRODUCES A GAS CALLED CARBON DIOXIDE. THIS GAS TRAPS HEAT FROM THE SUN, LEADING TO CLIMATE CHANGE.

Hydroelectric power plant

Renewable energy is energy that comes from any source that does not run out, for example solar (from the sun), wind, and tidal energy. Geothermal plants gather heat from the ground, which is used to make steam and <u>generate</u> electricity. Hydroelectric dams use the movement of water to power <u>turbines</u>. Nuclear power is made by something called fission. This involves splitting <u>atoms</u> of a material called uranium. As a renewable energy scientist, you might work for a company or for the government.

Renewable energy scientists develop ways of making renewable energy as useful as possible. As a wind energy scientist, for example, you might be involved in finding a windy location and working out how to position the wind turbines. You might also get involved in environmental issues, looking at ways to ensure a planned wind farm does not damage plant and animal life in the area.

As the need for energy grows, renewable sources such as solar power will become more and more important.

Renewable energy scientists work in the laboratory, in an office, and outside. Working outside could mean working in places that are hard to get to, and in all kinds of weather.

At a nuclear plant, you might work in a central control room like this.

In order to be a renewable energy scientist, you will need a science degree in a subject such as physics. Extra training in subjects such as climate science are also helpful. As well as your interest in science, clean energy, and the environment, you will also need great computer skills.

SPACE SCIENTIST

Does space fascinate you? Would you love to be a space traveler? Have you ever wondered how the universe began and whether there is life on other planets? If so, a career as a space scientist could be right for you. There are many different roles, from rocket designer to astronaut.

Some space scientists study space, including our own solar system and the billions of stars and galaxies that make up the universe. Some design <u>satellites</u>, spacecraft, and the equipment that they carry, then plan their launch into space. Others design test programs and experiments. They study data that is collected from satellites controlled on Earth. They also study results from experiments that have been carried out by astronauts on board spacecraft. Some work on projects exploring distant planets such as Jupiter, using remote control spacecraft and <u>probes</u>. Space scientists might also study the births, lives, and deaths of stars, planets, <u>asteroids,</u> and other objects in the universe.

A probe called Juno, controlled by a mission team at a space center, has explored Jupiter's atmosphere.

Some space scientists work as astronauts aboard the International Space Station (ISS). This is a spacecraft with people on it that <u>orbits</u> the Earth every 90 minutes. Its crew of three to six astronauts stay on board for about six months at a time. As well as carrying out all sorts of experiments inside the space station, the astronauts also go on space walks outside the spacecraft. The astronauts study how being in space for long periods of time affects the human body. They also clean, check, and repair equipment.

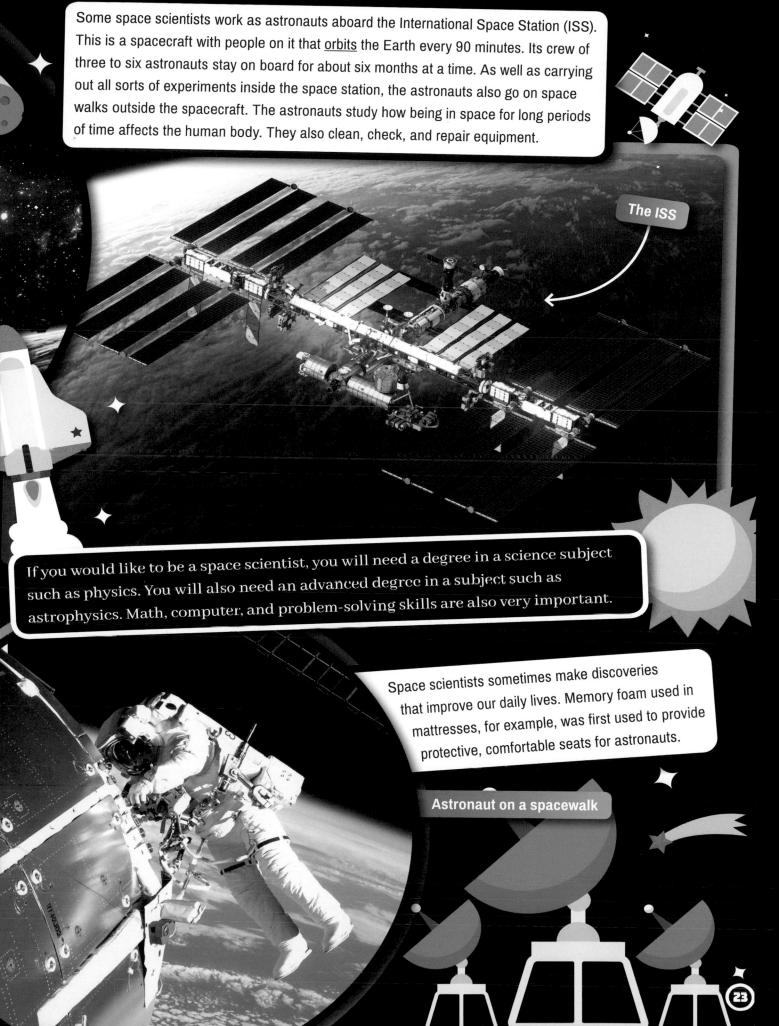

The ISS

If you would like to be a space scientist, you will need a degree in a science subject such as physics. You will also need an advanced degree in a subject such as astrophysics. Math, computer, and problem-solving skills are also very important.

Space scientists sometimes make discoveries that improve our daily lives. Memory foam used in mattresses, for example, was first used to provide protective, comfortable seats for astronauts.

Astronaut on a spacewalk

METEOROLOGIST

Meteorologists are scientists who study the Earth's climate and weather. They use all sorts of equipment and many scientific skills to record, understand, and forecast the weather. Meteorologists also study the causes of particular types of weather, such as hurricanes or tornadoes.

Meteorologists record and study information from worldwide weather stations, weather satellites, and weather balloons. They use this data, along with computer models, to forecast both short- and long-term weather patterns. Meteorologists also study the weather over long periods of time, looking at past weather trends to predict what the weather will be in the future.

Weather balloons carry special equipment that measures temperature, wind speed and direction, and the amount of water in the air.

IF YOU THINK THAT A CAREER IN METEOROLOGY IS FOR YOU, YOU WILL NEED A DEGREE IN SCIENCE, COMPUTER SCIENCE, MATH, OR METEOROLOGY.

This satellite is tracking a hurricane.

As a meteorologist, you might work for an environmental agency and research ways to cut down air pollution. You could be employed by a company that needs accurate weather information, such as an aircraft or energy company. You could also work in agriculture, helping crops grow by giving information on weather patterns and trends. A forensic meteorologist might work for companies that help people who have had accidents. This might involve looking at accidents that could have been affected by the weather.

As the effects of climate change continue to get worse, weather forecasting will become more and more important. Dry seasons, high temperatures, and strong winds, for example, lead to wildfires. These may put people, animals, and buildings in danger. Governments are employing more and more meteorologists to give expert advice on how to plan for and deal with climate change.

SPORTS AND EXERCISE SCIENTIST

If you enjoy science but are also passionate about sports, a career in sports and exercise science is for you. Sports and exercise scientists help people to improve their health and fitness. They can also help people to achieve the best possible results in their sport. They do this by using their knowledge of areas such as biomechanics (how the body moves) and physiology (how the body works).

There are many different roles in this field. You can work as a fitness consultant, checking people's fitness and putting together the right exercise program for them. If you work with athletes, you'll carry out tests to measure their performance. After studying the results, you'll design full training programs for them. Some sports scientists work in special medical centers, giving advice on how to treat sports injuries and stop them from happening in the first place. Others work with hospitals to help patients who need to become fit again, for example after a heart attack.

Measuring performance

Sports and exercise scientists work in many places. These include gyms and recreational centers, sports medical clinics, athletic training institutes, and professional clubs, such as soccer or ice hockey clubs.

Athlete

Some teach and carry out research in universities. Some work with sports companies, giving expert advice on how to design and make sporting equipment. Others set up their own clinics or work as personal trainers for people at home. You might be able to get work experience at a summer camp or a soccer academy.

If you would like to work as a sports and exercise scientist, you will need:

- a degree in sports and exercise science
- further training if you want to work in a particular area, such as nutrition (what food to eat for the best health and fitness)
- the ability to inspire people to work harder and exercise

Working as a volunteer for your local sports club can be rewarding. It can give you valuable work experience.

PHARMACIST

If you enjoy science and like the idea of giving people medicine to help them feel better, then a pharmacist could be a good career choice. But there is more to being a pharmacist than simply taking medicine from a shelf.

Pharmacists prepare, check, and package medicine that has been ordered by a doctor. It is the responsibility of a pharmacist to make sure the medicine is high quality and right for the patient. Pharmacists also check patients' symptoms and offer advice and over-the-counter medicine for illnesses such as coughs and colds. Over-the-counter medicines do not need a prescription (a prescription is a note from a doctor that says which medicine is needed). They also help people in other ways by giving them advice on how to live healthier lives. Pharmacists sometimes give advice about medicines to doctors.

Pharmacists work in many different places, including hospitals and community pharmacies. They might work for pharmaceutical companies that research, make, and sell medicine. Some work in prisons or in the armed forces. Some work at universities, either in teaching or research. Others train as veterinary pharmacists, providing care for animals.

This pharmacist is explaining the correct use of an asthma inhaler.

It takes around four years to complete a pharmacy degree. As a pharmacist, you will be dealing with lots of different people, including patients and doctors, so you will need to be good at talking to all sorts of people. An important part of the job is explaining to patients why they have to take a certain type of medicine. You will also explain how to take it safely and what the side effects might be.

You will need to be accurate and have an eye for detail, as the decisions you make can have a big impact on patients' lives. Things can get hectic, so you will need to be able to stay calm at all times.

Pharmacists have to keep detailed, accurate records.

SCIENTISTS WHO HAVE CHANGED THE WORLD

STEPHEN HAWKING

Stephen Hawking was a physicist and cosmologist (a scientist who studies the universe). He developed ideas about how the universe began and studied gravity and black holes. His popular science books helped ordinary people understand complicated ideas. Despite losing the ability to move and speak, he worked throughout his life, talking by using an electronic speech machine.

JACQUES COUSTEAU

Jacques Cousteau was an undersea explorer and marine conservationist (someone who looks after the environment). He co-invented the aqualung, a piece of diving equipment that helped divers stay underwater for long periods of time. His television documentaries opened up the undersea world to millions of viewers.

JANE GOODALL

Jane Goodall is a scientist who studied chimpanzees for nearly 60 years. She is a world expert, and her discoveries completely changed what we know about chimpanzees. She now works to protect the environment and make more people aware of the threats that chimpanzees face.

TU YOUYOU

Tu Youyou is a scientist who discovered medicine that was very good at fighting malaria. Malaria is a deadly disease that affects people all over the world. Tu Youyou's work has saved millions of lives. She won the 2015 Nobel Prize for Physiology or Medicine.

GLOSSARY

allergic reaction	the body's response to a substance that does not affect most people but causes some to feel unwell
asteroids	small, rocky objects that orbit the sun
atoms	the smallest possible parts of a chemical element
black holes	places in space where the pull of gravity is so strong that nothing, not even light, can escape
calories	units of measurement of the energy in food
climate change	a change in the typical weather or temperature of a large area
computer models	programs created on computers to test real-life situations
conferences	meetings of people with a shared interest that normally take place over several days
contamination	the act of making something unclean or unusable
databases	sets of data held in computers
degree	a qualification in a specialist subject, often given by a university or college to people usually over the age of 18
endangered species	groups of plants or animals that are at risk of extinction (being completely wiped out)
environmental agency	an organization that protects, manages, and conserves the natural world
evidence	proof
fossil fuels	fuels, such as coal, oil, and gas, which formed millions of years ago from the remains of animals and plants
fossils	the remains of prehistoric plants or animals that have been preserved in rock
generate	to create, produce, or make
gravity	the force that pulls everything downward toward the center of large objects in space
microbes	tiny organisms, such as bacteria, too small to be seen with the naked eye
microscope	a piece of scientific equipment used to make objects look many times bigger
nutritional value	the content of food, particularly protein, carbohydrates, and fat
orbits	repeatedly travels around another object in space in a curved path
pollution	something in the environment that has harmful or poisonous effects
probes	small spacecraft with nobody on board, sent into space to collect information and send it to scientists on Earth
research laboratories	rooms or buildings used by scientists to carry out experiments in order to discover new information
satellites	machines sent into space to orbit planets, take photographs, and collect and send information
specimens	individual animals, plants, or samples used for scientific study
turbines	machines with spinning blades for producing electricity
witnesses	people who see a crime take place and give evidence about it

INDEX

Photo Credits

Images are courtesy of Shutterstock.com. With thanks to Getty Images, Thinkstock Photo and iStockphoto.
2&3 – Glinskaja Olga, Victor Metelskiy, Anatolir, Arcady, DRogatnev, VOLYK IEVGENII, Marnikus, Jane Kelly, Idol Design, derter, Anna Frajtova, Nadya_Art, StockVector, tandaV, DRogatnev. 4&5 – sutlafk, michaeljung, Rido, Gorodenkoff, kotoffei. 6&7 – Richard Whitcombe, Bill45, zaferkizilkaya, Merla, Kzenon, Nadya_Art, Babka, Zubada. 8&9 – Monkey Business Images, Dragon Images, Liptak Robert, sqofield, H.Elvin. 10&11 – Sandra Matic, Couperfield, Vladimir Borovic, vchal, Anatolir, 12&13 – stockfour, Akimov Igor, Bildagentur Zoonar GmbH, kosmos111, karnoff. 14&15 – James Kirkikis, Aaronejbull87, Popova Valeriya, Incredible Arctic, Andrew Krasovitckii. 16&17 – Monkey Business Images, AimPix, wavebreakmedia, Halfpoint, artacet, DRogatnev. 18&19 – Hakim Yakoh, Gts, wavebreakmedia, Ekaterina_Minaeva, LEDOMSTOCK, Macrovector, angkrit. 20&21 – XXLPhoto, Maxim Burkovskiy, Mark Agnor, Nordroden, Mascha Tace, Amornism, St_art_ai. 22&23 – Vadim Sadovski, Dotted Yeti, 3Dsculptor, Artsiom Petrushenka, Graphiqa Stock. 24&25 – Shimon Bar, aapsky, FrameStockFootages, Christian Roberts-Olsen, Sea Owl, johavel. 26&27 – Gorodenkoff, Jacob Lund, takaimages, Rawpixel.com, Macrovector, Colorlife. 28&29 – wavebreakmedia, AS photo studio, all_about_people, i viewfinder, DRogatnev, AVA Bitter. 30 – The World in HDR, Hans Peters / Anefo [CC0], Tinseltown, Bengt Nyman [CC BY-SA (https://creativecommons.org/licenses/by-sa/4.0)].